THE REALTOR CODE

THE REALTOR CODE

Why Your Real Estate Career Is Slowly Dying And What You Can Do About It

MARK MACINERNEY

The Realtor Code: Why Your Real Estate Career Is Slowly Dying And What You Can Do About It Copyright © 2018 by Mark MacInerney.

All rights reserved. No part of this publication may be reproduced, distributed, or transmitted in any form or by any means, including photocopying, recording, or other electronic or mechanical methods, without the prior written permission of the author, except in the case of brief quotations embodied in critical reviews and certain other noncommercial uses permitted by copyright law.

Jones Media Publishing
10645 N. Tatum Blvd. Ste. 200-166
Phoenix, AZ 85028
www.JonesMediaPublishing.com

Disclaimer:
Information contained in our published works have been obtained by Jones Media Publishing from sources believed to be reliable from the author. However, Jones Media Publishing does not guarantees the accuracy or completeness of any information published herein and Jones Media Publishing shall not be responsible for any errors, omissions, or claims for damages, including exemplary damages, arising out of use, inability to use, or with regard to the accuracy or sufficiency of the information contained in this publication.

Printed in the United States of America.

ISBN-13: 978-1-945849-61-9 paperback

CONTENTS

Introduction 1

Chapter 1   Who Am I, and Why the Hell Should You Care? 5

Chapter 2   Loyalty and Trust ... Making Yourself Good for Business. 11

Chapter 3   Breaking the Procrastination Cycle 17

Chapter 4   Building Endurance. 23

Chapter 5   Creating Your Vision 29

Chapter 6   Cultivating Inner Strength. 41

Chapter 7   When Things Start Falling Apart 47

Chapter 8   Leveling Up. 53

Chapter 9   Don't Go Back to Being Normal 59

Chapter 10 A Scarcity Mind-set 65

Chapter 11 The Winning Play 71

Chapter 12 What the Future Holds for You 79

Conclusion: We Got This! 85

Quick Reference Guide 89

Introduction

For my realtors,

When I sat down to write this book for you, I had something else in mind. To be exact, it was a book about eating like a girl.

Now, I know what you're thinking: **Mark, what are you talking about?** A dieting book for realtors? Seems confusing, right? Well, let me give you a little bit of backstory.

My journey to write this book started with the idea of helping men have high-performance lives by eating like their wives or girlfriends. Before you bite my head off, I don't mean eating like a girl in the literal sense. The concept behind this philosophy was having discipline when you eat. I noticed that most women have this discipline naturally, where men need to work harder on mastering it. And then it hit me.

All success in life comes down to one thing: discipline. Whether you're dieting, working on your business, or developing a winning strategy in real estate, you won't get there without discipline. Some people seem to get there sooner than others, but that doesn't mean they're better set up for success than those who don't get there right away. If you've struggled with discipline in your life, there's still a chance for you. You can do this! All you have to do is be open and willing.

So now that we're on the same page, let's focus on what really matters: **How do you acquire discipline?**

Well, I'll teach you that! I'll teach you how to have more discipline in your life and your real estate business. That's a huge part of this book. But that's not what the *entire* book is about.

This book isn't about cultivating more success in your life. It can't be. I wrote this book to go beyond that.

You see, I have this belief. I believe **you're searching for something more**. Something that's been within your grasp but you haven't been able to capture. You're not gravitating toward the obvious signs of "success" in this industry. You're not chasing more commissions. You're not hunting for better buyers and sellers. And even if you mastered the art of discipline, you'd still want more.

Why do I believe this? Well, I've talked to tons of realtors about this business and what draws people to it, and every single conversation has gone in the same direction. "Mark, it's not success that people are after. No, it's more than that." When I ask for more clarification, I never get a straight answer, and it's different from person to person, but one thing is certain: everyone comes into real estate because they're after something beyond success.

Introduction

So, what exactly is it you're after, then? Well, that's where the discovery begins! This book is designed to start a conversation between you and me regarding just that. Real estate is a hard industry, and if you want to survive, you're going to need to make a few adjustments starting right now. You have to start thinking beyond the idea of success and be brave enough to go into territories unknown. Become open to the possibilities that may lie ahead for you in your career as an agent. You'll be surprised by what you find.

Before we dive deeper into discovery and the greater work, there are a few things I want to share with you:

The Codes

If you've been following me on Facebook or YouTube, you know I'm all about codes. Behind everything that runs smoothly in life is a code, and real estate is no different. Throughout this book, we're going to unlock the codes needed to discover what it is you're truly seeking and how real estate plays a role in that journey. And even though we're not going to call them codes in this book, the principle applies. In turn, you can use them to unlock more potential in your life.

The Challenge

There are professionals in this business who have "mastered" the real estate industry. If you've been in real estate for a while, you've met someone like this: someone who inspired you by their character and their ability to make magic out of thin air. They could do anything and sell anything in front of them. Any obstacle in their way was easily overcome.

These people, and the results they get, are hard to ignore. They emulate the very essence of what success is in our industry. But the problem is, if you watch them closely, it's almost impossible to pick out just one thing you can do to have what they have, be who they are, and go where they go.

It's okay to admire these people, but you have to understand something very important: that is their journey! You were designed to be the person you are, and you have the capacity to do what they do. And you're probably closer to getting the same results they are than you might think. But in order for you to get on the path to creating extraordinary results, you'll have to do the work outlined in this book.

So that's my challenge to you: **I challenge you to do the work. Don't worry about what other people are doing. Stay focused on what *you* should be doing.**

Make the Commitment

I'm going to teach you how to unlock the code to your true potential in life. However, I can't do this without you. You already showed me your commitment by buying this book. Now it's time to do the rest.

I'll show you how to create a life and business beyond what you think is possible, starting today. **But first, you have to open your mind and make a commitment to yourself that you won't give up.** Devote everything you've got to moving forward and be brave enough to begin.

And with that, let's begin!

1

Who Am I, and Why the Hell Should You Care?

AS YOU READ THIS BOOK, I'm sure you'll wonder, *Who is Mark MacInerney, and why the hell should I care?* Well, let me break it down for you.

I'm the guy who's going to help you realize stuff about yourself that you may be too afraid to believe or face. We all have things we're working on, stuff going on in our personal life and our business life. And this stuff either keeps us moving forward or holds us back. At times, it's easy to see what's going on and how it affects the way you do things. But at other times, it's hard to pinpoint what's creating all the problems and pitfalls.

The Realtor Code: Why Your Real Estate Career Is Slowly Dying And What You Can Do About It

You've had successes and failures in your life and in your business, but you're tired of riding that roller coaster. Now is the time to get off. This book will help with that.

I wrote this book for you, the realtor. I did this intentionally because as a mortgage broker, I've worked with tons of realtors over the years. And through my work with these realtors, one thing has become very clear to me: there's something seriously wrong with the real estate industry in general.

If you take a small step back from your desk, you'll see exactly what I see. All of us in the mortgage and real estate world are suffering from faulty relationships, lack of motivation, and a false idea of what success means. To most realtors, success means selling a bunch of houses, collecting a ton of money, and repeating the cycle until you can't do it anymore. And it's true—that can be a way to become successful—but I guarantee that it won't happen for you, at least not by following this pattern.

Real estate has become very complicated, not because of all the rules and regulations out there but because we simply don't trust ourselves or each other anymore. I do a training called "Everything Your Mortgage Broker Told You Is a Lie!" In this training, I open the eyes of both realtors and brokers to the amount of deception that goes on around us on a day-to-day basis. Realtors are working deals with brokers who are winning them over by stretching the truth, and realtors are only loyal to their mortgage person until they don't serve them anymore.

There's something wrong with this, right? Why is it okay for realtors and brokers to have so much mistrust between one another? Well, it's not. And that's why you should care.

Who Am I, and Why the Hell Should You Care?

As a realtor, you have a duty to yourself and everyone you meet to become the best version of yourself that you can possibly be. And you can't get there by having an unclear vision of who you are, what you stand for, and how you were designed to become successful in this business. That's what I care about.

I care about enhancing your character, both as a realtor and as a human being. You see, as a realtor, you have to be at your very best, not only for yourself but also for your clients. You've chosen to work in a field that can truly transform people's lives. The homeowners and potential homeowners you work with will be forever grateful to you when you make their dreams come true. That's a reward in and of itself, but it doesn't have to stop there. With the right tools and motivation, you can be rewarded in ways you didn't think were possible. That's what I'm offering you, and by accepting my offer, you're opening the door to reaching your true potential.

In order to open that door, though, you need some coaching. There's no way around it. Over the past year, I've been doing personal development through a program called "The Warrior's Way," and it was this program that opened my eyes to exactly what was going on in my life and how it was affecting my business. I'll never forget the moment everything came together for me. I was hitting my numbers and following the same "success" formula I mentioned before—sell a bunch of houses, collect a ton of money, repeat the cycle—but then it happened. I slowly started to fall.

Yes, I was still doing the work, but my life and my purpose faded away. I became the work, not realizing that the industry

The Realtor Code: Why Your Real Estate Career Is Slowly Dying And What You Can Do About It

had sucked me in. Nothing challenged me anymore. I was bored, but I still worked on my business and making money. Pretty soon, I was consumed by this notion of success, so much so that I became a Grade A asshole. No one could tell me anything—I knew everything. No one could reason with me—I was completely unreasonable. I was untouchable. Things seemed fine just the way they were.

On the outside, I played the game of the industry to keep my numbers up. I put up with the deceptions and inauthentic business practices because I thought I was supposed to. But on the inside, I had lost my purpose and my vision for what I truly wanted. I hated the way things ran in the real estate industry, and I wasn't shy about it, either. I told everyone I knew how I felt about real estate and mortgage lending, but I wasn't unhappy enough to quit selling houses or take a stand for what was right.

It took a family tragedy to break me down. It forced me to see the errors that bound me and people just like me to the illusion of "everything is okay." My wife was pregnant with our daughter, and I was in the midst of an affair. I was an alcoholic and treated my wife and kids like shit. Everything was about me. It had to be.

Then my daughter died. Out of the blue. One minute we were preparing for her arrival and then she was gone. And I was gone with her. I was ready for a divorce. I welcomed the freedom I thought I needed. I was the victim. "They're holding me back! They're robbing me of my greatest desires in life."

My life was a joke. I put up with things because it was easy—a lot easier than taking responsibility for my pain and what was truly going on. I settled in real estate because it was convenient. And through it all, I hit my numbers, which made me believe that everything was okay. I was okay, not great, and it was okay that I'd lost my way. I was surviving. But I was also completely empty, and that was okay, too. Well, it was until it wasn't anymore. But even then I didn't change because I had nothing to change for. That's when The Warrior's Way found me.

I'd always been tough. I'd always overcome any obstacle in my path. But this coaching program brought me down past the bottom and wouldn't let me settle for anything less than who I should have been all along. You see, the path I was on, the destiny I was fulfilling during my aimless walk, had brought me to the truth along the road. And it wasn't until I realized that I needed a process, a specific program, to help me redirect and course-correct that things started to really change. The Warrior's Way did that for me, and now I'll do that for you.

I, Mark, have set out to put these tools in front of you to build you up. It doesn't matter what you did yesterday or even today. I don't care if you're new to real estate or you've been in it for twenty years—either way, you need this! You need this book to remind you of what's important and what's at stake if you don't do the work. And you need this book because you're in real estate and our industry has a whole set of unique problems that you can solve.

I promise you, if you commit and do the work, together we'll carve out your greatness and separate you from the masses of realtors out there.

So there you have it. You know who you're dealing with: a mortgage broker who's on a quest to make your life and my life so much more fulfilling. Someone who has committed many "unforgivable sins." I've been there, done that. I've cut corners in life to try to be "great." But in the end, it wasn't until the light on the path showed me who I was becoming that I stopped to make a change. And it was then that my true greatness started to rise.

Now I'm looking for great realtors. Over the years, I've found some really good ones, but they've been few and far between. Now I need great ones. The industry needs great ones. And I know you're looking to be one of them or you wouldn't be reading this.

So let's do this! Let's get you on the path to greatness!

2

Loyalty and Trust ... Making Yourself Good for Business

BEFORE WE START ON THIS topic, I want to take a moment to thank *you*. As a realtor, you have a thankless job. When someone decides to buy a house, they get caught up in their dreams of owning a home. They feed off the potential memories they'll have in the house, and that hope creates a certain energy for them. Then comes the buying process.

Once the process starts, your buyers become relentless in their quest to get that house! They're full of emotions and the entire story surrounding the house, they forget that you're there to help them make their dream come true. And after the transactions are over, they move on to the next part of the home-buying process without remembering to thank you for all your hard work and dedication.

That's why I wanted to take this moment to say thank you for being an agent and selflessly taking care of our buyers. You're always appreciated.

A Day In the Life of a Realtor

Many agents get into realty because of the prospect of making so much money. However, those of us who have been in the industry for a while know exactly what this world is like. Before you can make a single dollar as an agent, you have to master the art of creating relationships with buyers, sellers, and other real estate professionals. This might sound like an easy task, but it's not.

When it comes to buyers and sellers, they tend to be focused on the process, so making a great impression comes down to adding value to the service. As we go along with this book, we'll talk more about how you can wow them by being a stellar agent.

For now, we're going to zero in on a problem everyone in real estate seems to have: lack of integrity.

The Obstacle: Lack of Integrity

In the world of real estate, there's no real reason why a realtor would pick a particular loan officer, inspector or agency over another. Everyone seems the same; their business models are almost identical. So when the contract comes in, realtors run through their rolodexes hunting for anyone who's available or who has the best rates.

This is a problem. When you jump around from agency to agency, mortgage house to mortgage house, you come off as wishy-washy. It's a complete turnoff. No one wants to do business with someone who doesn't stay true to them. And most important, when you are constantly moving from person to person, your deals suffer. You gain a reputation as a taker, so your "partners" don't feel comfortable giving you their best deals.

So, if you have this problem, how do you fix it? Well, you have to get to the core of the issue. Most realtors struggle with a tendency to be wishy-washy in their business life and their personal life. Think about it: when was the last time you felt scattered and sought to fix things by not really committing to anything? Not long ago, right? If we took a snapshot of your life, I bet we'd find other areas where this problem persists.

Look at your relationship with others. How often are you wishy-washy with your family and friends? When was the last time you kind of flaked off?

Look at your other interests and promises. When was the last time you went to the gym? Or how about budgeting and your finances—when was the last time you stuck to your budget or made an effort to stay on top of your finances?

Look at your overall goals. Everyone has goals, no matter how big or small they are. Did you set a goal to do self-development? Did you make a vow to drink less? Do you have a goal to make a certain amount of money? Whatever your goal is, when was the last time you achieved it? Are you even close?

The Realtor Code: Why Your Real Estate Career Is Slowly Dying And What You Can Do About It

Every day, people fall short in their relationships, their promises, and their goals. Why does this keep happening? Where does this problem come from? Lack of Integrity.

Most people think integrity just means being honest or moral, but integrity also means being undivided.

In real estate, the best way to be undivided is to be loyal and trustworthy.

The Solution: Loyalty and Trust

Being loyal as a realtor means building relationships with your power partners, clients, and anyone you do business with. Here are a few ways you can do that:

- **Focus on authenticity.** Being authentic is where loyalty and trust are born. As you grow your business, be conscious of who you are and what you stand for. If you work with other people in the industry who share your values, keep working with them. And find ways to support them in their business.

- **When you make a mistake, claim it and move on.** Trust is earned not only through what someone does but also through what they don't do. If you make a mistake, don't try to cover it up or lie about it. Instead, claim it, fix it, and move on. You'll get more business and better connections if you're known as someone who can take responsibility for your faults and who's a good problem solver.

- **Don't miss the details.** So many realtors rush through the process so they can close the deal and make money. Don't do this! Loan officers and inspectors notice when you pay close attention to the details. It helps make their job easier—and yours, too.

- Promote win-win situations. This one is huge. Win-win situations are the backbone of loyalty and trust. When you look for win-win situations, you're showing your intentions. And your intentions should promote relationships where your partners can come to you for support with their business needs. So they support you and you support them, and together you'll foster win-win situations.

Start Practicing Loyalty and Trust Today!

When you move away from being wishy-washy, you become a key asset to yourself and your team. This will build your confidence and your ability to remain loyal and trustworthy. Below are some practices you can do every day to continue cultivating loyalty and trust:

- Don't break promises, not even to yourself. If you say you're going to do something, do it. And if you can't, be truthful about it.

- Examine your goals. Do your goals support loyalty and trustworthiness? If not, you need to adjust them until they do.

- Make authenticity your number one priority. No matter what situation you're in, always stay true to who you are and your values.

- Own up to your mistakes and fix them. Don't overthink your mistakes. Just solve the problem and move on.

- **Don't miss the details.** Put a lot of emphasis on doing a great job and keeping your business clean. Be careful when making deals, and always do the right thing.

- **Always create win-win situations.** This is by far the most important practice. Whether it's business or your personal life, always promote win-win situations. (We'll cover this more in a later chapter.)

Remember, Money Won't Solve This Problem for You!

Many people go into real estate with hopes and dreams of making a ton of money. They have this notion because they need the money. They believe that money will solve their problems. This is not true! Yes, money is a resource that can help you in your personal life and business, but it won't solve the fundamental issues in your business. Start by being more loyal and trustworthy. This will cure some of the most basic problems you're having in your business, I promise. Once that's done, you'll create stronger relationships, which will take you far in this industry.

3

Breaking the Procrastination Cycle

SO, WE'VE COVERED BEING TRUSTWORTHY and being loyal in your business and your personal life. By developing these two crucial characteristics, you'll be able to create better relationships with your partners and your clients. However, being loyal and trustworthy is only the beginning. There's much more you need to strengthen on the inside. In this chapter, we're going to talk about something that most realtors and people in general struggle with: procrastination.

Procrastination and the Realtor

The way procrastination affects realtors is different from the way it affects other types of business owners. Unlike other industries, real estate actually breeds laziness. Why is that? Money and prospecting.

Why Potential Wealth Can Make Realtors Lazy

Realtors are constantly told about the amount of money they can make on just one transaction. If you make 3 percent commission on a $500,000 home, you're making $15,000 on that transaction alone. If you sell one house a month, you're walking away with $180,000 a year. Now, can you imagine selling a million-dollar home? If you sold one house a month for $1 million, you're looking at $360,000 a year!

So, realtors try to sell one large contract a month because it will make them incredibly rich one day! This logic is the breeding ground for laziness—if you sell one house a month, you don't have to do anything else. But that isn't true. Selling real estate takes time, and the more deals you have going, the better.

Problems with the Prospecting Game

When you become a realtor, your main goal is to learn about selling houses and finding people to buy them. The best place to start is with your natural market: your friends and family. But this approach has some serious drawbacks.

Doing deals with your friends and family sets you up for unrealistic expectations. Working with people you know gives you the belief that real estate transactions are easy and prospects come in large troves. This isn't true! As I said in the last chapter, people want to work with individuals they like and trust. In this day and age, it takes some time for anyone to trust you. While your prospects are learning to trust you, you're not making any money off the deal. It's only when contracts are signed, approved, and completed that you'll see a dime.

So, yes, working with your friends and family is a great way to start, but remember, it will take strong relationships to get you in the top ranks as a realtor. And there's only one way to do that: you have to build a successful business.

Building a Successful Business

Believing you're going to make tons of money gives you the impression that you'll have tons of money to spend on increasing your lifestyle. Don't fall for this trap! Even if you're lucky enough to have deals come in and turn over quickly, you need to put money back into your business. As an agent, you can invest in your business by hiring a coach.

I know what you're thinking. "How is a coach going to help me with my real estate business?" Coaching gives you a set of goals that help you to be accountable. They also break the Cycle of Unhealthy Realtor Habits.

Breaking the Cycle

Realtors have picked up a few horrible habits over the years: procrastination, unrealistic expectations, and chasing easy money. These three things create a cycle that, like a tornado, sucks up all your opportunities and destroys them. But you can overcome this by breaking the cycle early on in your business.

Do the small stuff. Start by proving that you can do the small stuff. Everybody wants to make easy money, but they aren't willing to do the hard stuff to get there. If you start with the small stuff, you'll be able to handle the bigger stuff later. A few small things you can do now are getting up early, eating consistently and well, avoiding excessive drinking, and getting to bed early. These simple lifestyle tweaks will help you stay in the game long enough to make some serious money.

Stay motivated. Procrastination comes from focusing too much on the big stuff. By starting with the big stuff, you're making it harder for you to be accountable to these big goals. This is where motivation comes in. Motivation builds up when you can first handle having a day-to-day routine that you've mastered. It's your foundation. A sturdy one. Then, when you move up to the bigger stuff, you'll have the motivation to take it on.

Focus on self-discipline and gratitude. Doing the small stuff and staying motivated gets you self-discipline. It's this self-discipline that brings you the energy that propels you into the bigger deals because it creates gratitude. You see, we're energy-based beings. When we carry negative energy around, it hurts us in our business and personal lives. But if you do the small stuff, stay motivated, and focus on self-discipline, your attitude and energy will be positive and reflect gratitude.

Don't feel entitled. Receiving referrals from your family and friends is always a blessing, but it's not your livelihood. Getting new business in the door is hard work but well worth it. As you grow your business and become a stronger agent, you open yourself up to lots of opportunities; you increase your chances of making it across the finish line. Entitled agents don't experience that. Agents who think something is owed to them just because they passed the test won't make it in this business, I promise. It doesn't matter how many natural market connections you have—if your clients sense that they "owe" you their business, they'll take it somewhere else, guaranteed.

Break the Cycle, Now!

Start with the small stuff! Tonight, you can get a good night's sleep and start tomorrow with a new direction. Make those changes and stay motivated. And remember, don't feel entitled!

Learn as much as you can by hiring a coach who can help you grow and keep you accountable. It'll make a huge difference and save you tons of time.

You're a great agent. You have the power to go out there and make a great life for yourself.

4

Building Endurance

MOST REALTORS JUMP INTO REAL estate for the long haul. They dream of starting out as an agent, moving over to the lending side, buying up some properties for retirement, and moving to some tropical island with stacks of cash. Well, some of that is true.

Real estate is one of the most lucrative industries to be in, due to the fact that everyone everywhere will need a place to live. And if you play your cards right, the supply-and-demand aspect of real estate will always keep potential buyers and sellers calling you. But in order to enjoy the benefits of having a long life in real estate, you first have to build up endurance.

Building Up Endurance

One of the major differences between successful and unsuccessful realtors is endurance. Endurance is the building block of meeting challenges.

When I was training for my triathlon, my first step toward completing the race was making the decision to complete it. I envisioned myself crossing the finish line, having accomplished something that was great for my body and would create positive change in all the aspects of my life. Once I did that, I got to work—immediately.

I focused on all the preparations and training I would have to do in order to complete the race. And, of course, I hired a trainer to help me through it all. When we had our first meeting, I was in the game, I was ready. And then the workouts began.

I worked out hard and put everything I had into it, but that first workout killed me. And so did the next one. And the one after that.

But nevertheless, I continued to train because I knew every mile I ran, every swim I did, every weight I pushed was building up my endurance. As I got stronger, as my body became unstoppable, my endurance grew with it. And when I completed the race, it showed. I wasn't the same person anymore. At the beginning, I was an unsuccessful athlete who had just enough determination and heart to squeak through challenges, but by the end of my race, I had turned into a warrior with the endurance to take on everything in my path. It was an incredible feeling not only because I'd accomplished something I set out to do but also because it helped my business grow.

When Endurance and Dedication Meet

The moment you start working on your endurance, your dedication to things will start to rise. This is a direct result of making a commitment to yourself. When I was training for my race, I made an unconditional commitment to my success. You see, success isn't a money thing—it's a mind-set thing. And that mind-set is tied to dedication.

When you're in the right mind-set, you'll be dedicated to yourself and the people you work with, which leads to success. I've met realtors who thought that changing mortgage bankers would help them to do better. This isn't true. How are you going to have a great business if you're not dedicated?

There's no transition for going from being a broke agent to being a rich one. You have to start with dedication, and you have to press "start" today! Start doing the things in this book. Be dedicated to yourself and those around you. It will make all the difference in your business.

Creating a Strong Work Ethic

So, you've got endurance and dedication down, but there's still one more thing you need in order to be successful: a strong work ethic. When I started out as an agent, I knew I was going to be successful because of my strong work ethic. I got very clear on what I was supposed to be doing, and I got to work. And soon enough, I started solving problems for many other agents, too.

The Realtor Code: Why Your Real Estate Career Is Slowly Dying And What You Can Do About It

I realized that other agents could benefit from an "I'm willing to do what it takes, regardless" attitude. This comes in very handy, especially when someone tries to tell you it can't be done. Remember, these people are just coaching from their perspective. Look at what they do and how well they're doing it. I guarantee you'll have your own perspective on the best way to do it. And that becomes your work ethic.

A strong work ethic begins when you accept the challenge and know you can do it. If you're not sure if you can do it, do it anyway. The moment you tell yourself you can do it, your mind will shift and you'll see the possibilities. These possibilities strengthen your work ethic because you become someone people want to work with and under. And if the possibilities don't exist yet, create them! So many people think they'll develop these skills once the opportunities rise, but that's completely backward.

You have to show your work ethic by doing things that are uncomfortable for you. This will show your dedication to the project, yourself, and your team. To truly impress people, continue doing the project or task for a week or two. Here are a few things you can do to demonstrate your work ethic:

- **Prospecting.** Agents want listings, but they don't do enough prospecting to get them.
- **Follow-ups.** Got leads on your desk? Call them! Most of your money will be lost if you don't follow up with your prospects.
- **Following through.** This is different from following up. If you say you're going to do it, do it—and get it done early. If you say you're going to be there, show up early.

Be the agent who's known around the office for having the strongest work ethic. Be the agent your clients brag about to their friends because they know how dedicated you are!

One last thing: work ethic and accountability go hand in hand. If you're not accountable to both the big and the small goals in your business, you'll have problems. And you can't blame these problems on anyone else or the company. So stay focused and be accountable to your word!

Making Sound Business Decisions

This might seem like a strange topic for a chapter on endurance, but trust me, sound business decisions are exercised over time. If we were to take a look at your business right now, would we find that you have enough money to pay your taxes? Is your marketing budget reasonable? What's your five-year plan? How close are you to achieving your next goal? These are all things that come into play when you're working your business.

Sound business decisions keep your business alive and give it the endurance to withstand any market. Right now, I want you to take the steps on the following list:

- Look at your schedule. How much of your day is spent doing what?
- Check on your goals. What goals have you set for the year? When will you achieve them?
- Track your expenses. Are you spending too much money on this and not enough money on that?

- Plan your next move. What's the next move in your business? Why did you choose this action, and how will it benefit you?

There are a lot of realtors out there who have no clue what's going on behind the curtain of their business. You need to know these things! It's imperative that you keep managing your day-to-day activities so you can make better decisions in your business.

Endurance Breathes Life Into Your Business

Your business can withstand anything if you cultivate endurance inside yourself. So, build up your endurance, become dedicated to your business, and develop a strong work ethic!

5

Creating Your Vision

OUR NEXT TOPIC IS PROBABLY the most important thing you'll learn in this entire book: creating a vision.

Having a vision is beyond empowering. When I started my journey to becoming more enlightened, I thought I'd figured everything out. I knew what I was supposed to be doing and why I was doing it. But then the clarity started to fade, and I began seeking the path to becoming realigned with my purpose. However, the gift I received was so much more than that.

I went to Cleveland to help a buddy of mine with an event he was putting together. The event was designed to help people build their self-esteem and confidence. As I sat there supporting my friend and the attendees, I felt something shift within me. I had this power come over me, and I was able to use that power to deliver light into people's lives. I could help people, just like you. But, I wasn't ready. I had to create a vision first.

Creating a Vision

At the beginning of my search, I walked around with a specific vision for my life and my business. At the moment, I had a pretty strong regime going: training for my triathlon, participating in my coaching, staying centered with my family, and killing it in my business. Everything was done in ninety-day challenges: ninety days to train for and complete my triathlon, ninety days to get my business in order, etc. Every day, every week, I was accomplishing something. And each challenge I finished felt great. The empowerment flowed through me.

Then it stopped. Something was up—I could sense it. That's when the signs started showing up.

As I prepped for my triathlon, a voice crept in, telling me to take a break. So I took a step back, which allowed me to see that if I took time away from my challenges and stepped away from coaching for a bit, I would find what this enlightenment was trying to tell me. I could focus my energy into a creative channel.

And that's what I did. I stepped down from my coaching, put my training on hold, and went into the abyss of channeling my creativity. As I focused, a message came through: significance. **I wanted to be significant to people.** I wanted my purpose to center on bringing my significance into people's lives. This made total sense.

Creating Your Vision

In real estate, we play a significant role in helping families and individuals get a house. We make dreams come true literally every day. And it's through this process that our significance grows. It was the perfect starting point!

For a few days, I grew this idea. I fostered it constantly until I arrived at my own coaching program that would add value to my mentees and to me. At that point, I decided to share my new insight and direction with my coaching buddies. I was pumped! I was ready for them to confirm my discoveries. But their feedback led to a startling revelation.

"Mark, your absence from the group has really thrown things off. You have to be more accountable to your commitments and how you show up in your life."

This led to a conversation—a deep, angry conversation. I made it clear to them that my enlightened journey had given me a chance to create something of significance. Through the work I was going to do, I would change many lives. But they didn't see it that way. Throughout our conversation, all they heard was how much "I" wanted to make a difference. "I" had to be significant. **It wasn't about the people I could help—it was all about me.**

I had to admit it to myself: I was wrong. My ego had shown up, a selfish part of me that had sneaked into my intentions. Yes, I did want to help people, which was a noble task, but I had to go about it a different way. I considered their feedback and made a huge course correction. To get my vision together, I had to start by learning about humility.

Looking for a Vision and Finding Value

My quest to be significant brought me face-to-face with a value, and that value was rooted in humility. I couldn't do anything, including writing this book, without seeking humility first. Once I accepted this, I could lay the groundwork for my vision.

When you start your vision planning, you have to begin with the value you want to bring. As a realtor, you have to ask yourself, "How does value play a role in my day-to-day life?"

Realtors can put such a negative connotation on what they do. They slog around, showing houses with little energy, and bring a sense of struggle to the job. This is deadly. Negative energy only breeds more negativity, and now is not the time to be off your game.

Building your business without value will put you in a dying role. With today's technology, the need for a realtor is starting to dwindle. Buyers can go online and look at houses. Mortgage companies make getting preapprovals super-easy. So where do you stand now? How will you survive? By adding value. Build your vision on this.

Step 1: Adding Value by Staying Connected

Staying connected comes down to being relevant. When you aren't connected to the deal, the buyer feels it, the seller feels it, and the money reflects it. This will create discomfort for you, which leads to feeling negative about your job. Your negativity then pollutes your energy and your income is affected. It's all connected. So if you stay connected in the process, you'll open your energy to possibilities. Put this in your vision: "How will I add value?"

Step 2: Get Clear on What You Want

"I want money! The end." This is what most entrepreneurs and realtors focus on. But this means absolutely nothing. You have to really evaluate what you want to receive and how you plan to get there. In my experience, whatever it is you're chasing should bring about a win-win situation for you and the people you're working with. For example, your buyer has a very specific want, and when you look at this want, you have to be honest with yourself: can you deliver for this client?

When money is your only motivation, you'll do whatever you can to make this work, even if it means you don't completely know what you're doing. This doesn't create a win-win situation for your clients. Instead, get very clear on what you want and how you can add value through your talents and abilities. This will allow you to service your client and accomplish something within your vision.

Step 3: Practice Gratitude

Let's say you encounter a problem you can't solve, and instead of taking it on, you decide to give the client a referral to someone you know. Some realtors look at this situation as counterproductive, but that's not the case. Giving referrals should be part of your overall vision. When you give referrals or share commissions, you're operating from a space of gratitude. And in real estate, we need to practice gratitude every day!

Think about it: being a giver in this industry helps both the buyer and the seller in the long run. Some realtors shy away from this principle because they want to chase "fake money." They sit at their desks calculating out how much they'll earn if the deal goes through. They conduct business with others based on protecting the prospect of getting this money. But they fail to realize that the money doesn't exist until the deal closes.

So when you create your vision, don't leave gratitude out. Don't get protective about money that doesn't belong to you. Flourish in the moment right now, and stay away from making a commitment to chasing these types of deals. Remember, the more you support others in this business, the more they'll want to show their gratitude to you.

Step 4: Start Saying No

Creating a vision allows you to ask the universe for whatever you want. And the moment you ask for a vision, purpose, and value, the gates will open up, allowing you to receive whatever it is you're looking for. When this happens, you'll feel a wave of emotions, most of which will be positive. And in the midst of all this positivity, you'll want to say yes to everything.

A buyer wants you to travel out of your area to show them a house—you say yes! A referral wants you to give up more commissions for a deal that "might" go through—you say yes! You say yes because things are going great and you want to open up more opportunities. But the truth is, by saying yes you're actually giving up your chances of making more money and providing more value. If you want to protect your vision, you have to say no.

Saying no shouldn't be considered a negative. It's a positive thing. Your vision will help with that. Your vision should contain only the things that move your business and your life forward. So when an opportunity comes, check it against your vision. If it's not part of your vision, say no.

Step 5: Add Coaching to Your Vision

Once you figure out what you want to put in your vision, hire a coach. Coaching is imperative. It's too valuable to live without. We need structure. Just like children, we need a routine in order to grow and continue reaching our objectives. Coaching is the only way to keep things going. It's there to point out things we haven't noticed in ourselves.

Not sure if coaching is a necessity for you? Well, I'll tell you, none of the greatest athletes, business owners, or leaders got where they are by doing things alone. Remember, these people are just like you and me. They didn't always want to struggle, either, but they got through it by leaning on someone else who kept them accountable.

When you hire your coach, they'll help you construct your vision. But in the meantime, I'll give you an outline to help you get started.

Vision Construction

My enlightenment journey created a pattern interruption. It changed up my routine and threw everything into a loop.

Because of this, I was able to hold space for creativity and grow my vision with humility. This was my revelation, but that doesn't mean you have to follow in my footsteps to a T. Your journey is different, and your vision will be different. Here's how you can start constructing your vision:

Create a Vision for Each Area of Your Life

I'm a huge fan of breaking up a vision into ninety-day challenges. Each ninety-day challenge is centered on an area of your life. To keep it simple, we can divide your life into four major sections: your body, your mind, your purpose, and your business.

Vision: Your Body

Your body is your temple. It gives you power and strength to make things happen. I recommend setting up a ninety-day challenge to increase your daily activities. Also include a healthy eating plan. Part of this healthy eating means cutting out anything that might be holding you back. Do you need to quit smoking? Is drinking a problem for you? Cut it out. Trust me, when you get into the full-throttle zone, you'll need a strong body and all the energy you can get.

For the next ninety days, I want you to make being healthy a priority. Be conscious of what you eat. Move your body at least thirty minutes a day. Do something every day that will push you a little further than you went the day before.

Creating Your Vision

Vision: Your Mind

I once heard someone say that your mind-set as a business owner says a lot about the type of business you have. As a realtor, your business can seem scattered. You have to drive buyers around town, keep track of your CRM, work with other professionals, etc. Managing all this can make it hard to keep your mind straight. This is where mental toughness comes in.

A great ninety-day challenge is focusing on building your mental toughness. I recommend diving deep into setting goals that pertain to prospecting, learning more about our industry, and money management.

- **Prospecting:** You can set a goal every morning to meditate for a few minutes to wrap your mind around this idea of prospecting. As you meditate, remind yourself of what value you bring to the table. Focus on the positive, not the negative. When you do this, it will take away the stress of having to put yourself out there.
- **Continued learning:** Interest rates will change, and buyers will notice. Housing demands will increase and decrease, and sellers will notice. Everything that happens in our industry will affect you and your clients. As a realtor, your job is to continue learning as much as you can. Your knowledge of the industry will give your clients confidence and improve your mental toughness around an ever-changing real estate climate.
- **Money:** Believe it or not, you need mental toughness surrounding money. It's easy to make tons and tons of money—managing it is the hard part. Your challenge

for the next ninety days is to pay close attention to your money. What are you spending your money on? How much money are you putting toward your business? What types of expenses do you have? How can you manage your money better? Be mindful of your money every day. A small change can be the big difference between riches and poverty.

Vision: Purpose

Think about your purpose every day. Challenge yourself to go deep. You're more than just a realtor; you do more than just "sale houses." You bring something special to the table, something unique. And that should be the driving force for your vision.

For the next ninety days, I want you to live each day with purpose and intention. Explore what that really means for you. What do you gravitate toward? What thoughts and ideas constantly recur for you? These might be indicators to what your purpose is.

Finding your purpose will change how you approach your day. When I figured out that coaching people was part of my purpose, I began structuring my daily activities around developing that skill. All my training and energy went into growing into the person I needed to be as a coach.

Keep a journal of your thoughts and record details about your day. As you review your content, look for differences between where you were before and where you are now. People who live every day with a purpose tend to do much better than those who don't.

Vision: Business

Your vision for your business is parallel with your vision for your life. If you get your body strong, build your mental toughness, and find your purpose, everything will align in your business, guaranteed.

For the next ninety days, keep your work and your life balanced. Stay focused on bringing your passion through in everything you do. Don't get distracted. Don't let other people tell you who you should be and what your vision should look like. You picked this industry for a specific reason. And you're here with a specific purpose. Your business will thrive through your vision.

Moving Forward

By now you should be excited about creating a vision for yourself. You'll be amazed by how much easier your life and business will be once you create your vision and implement it. But remember, you can't do it alone.

Don't forget to add coaching to your top priorities. I offer coaching programs for realtors and individuals who want to take things to the next level. If you want to get connected with me to learn more about how we can work together, I've included all my contact information at the end of this book.

6

Cultivating Inner Strength

WE MOVE THROUGH LIFE TAKING on challenges. Some challenges are more intense than others. For realtors, our main challenges are prospecting and getting deals to close. It's a grind, and if you're not careful, it'll suck all your energy dry.

I've gone through it. I've been in plenty of situations where success seemed far out of reach. Everything took too much work, and I felt like I got nothing in the end. But did I give up? No! I turned my focus from the external to the internal. I used my inner strength to see me through.

Inner Strength is for the Road

When you throw yourself into challenges, your expectation makes you believe you'll be different once you hit the top. And it makes sense. The person you were while going through the challenge had to change in order to get to the top. You had to evolve, shift things around, and make new commitments in order to ascend upward. But suddenly you're at the top and nothing has changed. You feel great and the journey has made you stronger, but you plateau. Why does this happen? Your inner strength has left you.

We need inner strength to get us from Point A to Point B, and when you get to the peak, you don't need that strength anymore. Realtors experience this constantly. You close a deal, one you've been working hard on, and then the commission comes in. You get excited and revel in the money you earned, and then the feeling goes away. You have to start over again. And this thought leaves you feeling unfulfilled.

You've lost your inner strength. You've lost the one thing that kept you going. How did that happen? Well, it's simple—the journey was over. The struggle wasn't needed anymore. When this happened, your inner strength diminished with it. And if you want to get it back, you'll have to cultivate inner strength constantly.

What Is Inner Strength?

In my definition, inner strength is believing in yourself. When you believe in yourself, it doesn't matter what happens. Whatever comes your way, you'll have faith in yourself and your situation, and you know you'll see it through to the end.

Cultivating Inner Strength

The Mirror Game

We're given so many mirrors in life that it can be a negative thing. You put something out there and the world shows it back to you, and what you see can be hard. With inner strength, no matter what you see, you'll have the ability to move forward. You can persevere. You will be who you are, without having to apologize for it.

Cultivating Inner Strength

Cultivating inner strength starts with confidence. The more confidence you have, the easier it will be to build your inner strength. Look at Olympian athletes. They move away from society to train for four years straight so they can become the most elite person on Earth in their particular sport. And when their race or competition comes up, the gold medalist wins by less than a second. In some cases, it's a tenth of a second. That's it.

So, what gives winners that slight advantage? Inner strength. They create a level of confidence that pushes them forward. And you can use this same approach in your business. Increase your level of confidence by doing things you're good at every day. Focus on those things. Grow them. Then start taking your confidence to another level by getting better at things you're not good at or things you don't want to do. It's about the small stuff.

What are a few small things you keep neglecting to do in your business? Calls? Prospecting? Working on listings? Acing these things could give you more confidence. Imagine it: doing prospecting calls until you have a new sense of ease around them. Or going out of your way until you feel comfortable with every part of doing your business. If you do these things, your confidence will go sky high.

Confidence and arrogance. When you start working on your confidence, two roads will be presented to you, one leading to humility and one to arrogance. When you pick humility, you and everyone on your team will win. If you choose arrogance, your future will be destroyed before you even begin.

If you find yourself becoming arrogant, look at your ego. Your ego is attached to fear. When you give in to this fear, you fall out of your natural state, which is love and kindness. As long as you're in your ego, you won't be able to share positivity with others. This will hurt your business. So let it go. Your ego will bring you nothing in life.

Start a twelve-month journal. When you're on the road to where you're going, the progress you'll make will seem slow and minimal. However, it's the slow, small stuff that will get you through to the end. As you build inner strength, your journal will help you stay motivated. It will encourage you to see the changes.

But before you start your journal, I want you to write yourself a letter. Your transformation starts today by writing out who you are. What are your hopes and dreams? What's holding you back? What are you doing? Write about it. Write everything you can think of. Write about your relationships, the good ones and the bad ones. Be honest about where you are in your business. Don't leave anything out. And when you finish with that, close your letter with your expectations and goals.

Put this letter away and plan to open it one year from today. And in the meantime, journal about your days. Capture all the things that happen in your business. After a while, you'll realize that you're stronger than you thought.

Focus on longevity. Inner strength is a longevity game, especially for us in the real estate world. If you've been in the game for ten years or more, you've already encountered inner strength. This isn't an easy business—it's incredibly competitive—and those who are still here should pat themselves on the back for sticking it out.

Use your longevity as a superpower. Consistently grow each year. Stay active in your role, even if you've been doing it for a long time. And while you're doing your work, stay loyal to those who help you. Remember, they've shown longevity with you, so return the favor to them.

The Missing Finish Line

In this industry, you'll have short-term and long-term goals, and you may not be able to see the finish line. So live every day to the fullest. Your life could be purposeful by meeting your challenges and growing from them. What you accomplished during the journey was the fulfillment of meeting each goal and the prospect of meeting goals in the future. You can do this. You already have!

7

When Things Start Falling Apart

THERE COMES A MOMENT IN every realtor's career when things will go absolutely perfectly. The referrals will come in nonstop. Your commissions will bring in tons of money. All your hard work will pay off. And you'll be completely unstoppable.

These are the moments we live for. It's why we put ourselves through the pain: the mountaintop. From there, all you can see is miles and miles of opportunities. With things going this great, it's hard to imagine things becoming a struggle again. But they will.

Some of your transactions will fall apart. This usually happens when you place too much of your trust in certain brokers or real estate professionals. In some cases, you may not know exactly why the deals didn't work out. In the end, you just go on with your business and hope it never happens again. And then it does.

The truth is, mortgage lenders may not be completely transparent about what goes on in lending. They don't always do their jobs, and some can be complacent. So it's your job to do everything right for yourself, your buyers, your sellers, and your transactions. And when things get off track, you have to fix them—quickly. Here's what you need to do when things start falling apart.

Evolution and Framework

When things aren't working out, you'll probably notice that things don't seem right. It doesn't happen in a day. As things slowly begin to fall out of alignment, you need to evolve, and you have to do it quickly. If you start a deal with a broker and they aren't doing their part, end it immediately. Get a second opinion. Find someone else.

The framework for your business should include having strong mortgage lenders. A strong lender is someone who makes sure you get a preapproval letter. They help you make sure everything goes through on the purchase side. This keeps the deal from falling apart. But it's not the only thing.

Inside your business, you should build a strong foundation. This foundation is a combination of learning and skill. When you learn, you understand the process inside and out. Nothing comes as a shock to you. From here, you can keep yourself from being taken advantage of.

Don't Let Anyone Take Advantage of You

It's imperative that real estate agents know the mortgage side. Period. Start learning it now. If you do, you'll add tons of value to people on both sides of the transactions. And when buyers and sellers go online to do their own research, they'll know you truly want the best for them. Guaranteed.

Adding value to your clients and your transactions will put you ahead of the rest, but doing a good job can also put a target on your back. There are some people out there who will want to take advantage of you. Don't let them. You can use "framework" to keep you moving forward without the threat of someone taking something from you.

Setting a frame. When you start a deal, set the frame on how things need to go. Let the buyers and sellers know what needs to happen, how it needs to happen, and when things should be completed. People operate well in this environment because it sets boundaries; your job is to keep these boundaries and enforce them.

Enforcing boundaries. Do you run around town with your clients looking at houses even if they don't really know what they want? Do you allow your clients to move through the process at their own pace? This happens often. Your clients don't know what's going on in the deal and this creates problems in the transaction and with boundaries. You can overcome this by being a great realtor and setting the proper outcomes for your clients. Here are a few boundaries you can set today:

- **Preapprovals.** Your buyers must get preapproval before you go out to look at houses. This is in their best interest and yours. There's no reason for you to spend your value time looking at houses if your clients can't afford them.
- **Proper documentation.** Waiting on clients to provide documentation is a nightmare. And it brings deals to a halt. Make sure that your clients are on the path to success by producing the right paperwork early in the process. This will take a load off them and make the process go more quickly.
- **Expectations.** Your clients have specific wants and needs for their new house, and you should know what they are. By setting a boundary around expectations, you'll cut down on the guesswork.

Benefits of creating boundaries. When you start using boundaries and frames, it will show you exactly what type of relationship you have with your client. If the boundaries are uncomfortable for your client, they'll leave, which isn't a bad thing. You don't want to work with a client who isn't willing to honor and respect your need to move the process forward.

Boundaries also keep you from being a dictator. Allow your clients an opportunity to roam around in the boundaries you create. If they have a valid reason for pushing the boundary a little, let them. If you give them that freedom, they'll be better clients and more willing to move the process forward with more urgency.

Getting the Proper Guidance

Structure will help your clients, but it will also help you. Without structure and boundaries, things get delayed, including your growth. If you put framework around things, you'll get whatever you want. So put your frame into the parameters that help you stay focused and get things done. To help you do this, you'll need to hire a coach.

Real estate doesn't offer any structure. You make all this money, but no one holds you accountable for your time. So you waste it. Tons of it. A coach can help you with this. When you get a coach, you get a regime, and through this regime you make more money and become a better agent. This is far better than the alternative: going it alone.

Sometimes, we need help locating the solutions within us. When you go through coaching, you'll have someone who's a positive influence on you. They'll take you from where you were to where you want to be. And when they do, you'll realize you already had everything you needed to succeed. All the coaching did was give you the opportunity to bring these things to the surface.

Now, this may seem strange, but I'm going to end this chapter with a "coaching call-out." If you're not in coaching right now, you need to be. The dreams you have won't be achieved if you don't hire a coach. A coach will put you on the right path, give you encouragement, and help you succeed, guaranteed.

So don't put it off. Put structure into place in your life and your business—hire a coach. Give me a call or send me a text or an e-mail and let's get you set up with someone who can help!

8

Leveling Up

THE LONGER YOU'RE IN REAL estate, the easier things will become. You'll eventually understand your buyers and sellers so well that you'll be able to anticipate their next move. When commission checks come in, you'll smile, knowing you did a great job. Every deal that comes into your office will be pretty much the same: work with the buyers and sellers, sign the documents, and move on to the next.

As a new realtor, you got excited for these moments. The moments when things make complete sense. Then you become more knowledgeable, so you try to hit bigger targets. Instead of selling a $500,000 home, you shoot for a $1 million home. You put all your time and focus into making the biggest deals happen. But you find yourself chasing your own tail. You're not making any progress anymore, and your pipeline dries up. What happened?

Your priorities were in the wrong place. You tried to go too far. And it's not your fault. Wanting to hit big goals is human nature, but these big goals will get you off track. If you want to hit it big in real estate, you have to start leveling up in your business.

Leveling Up is a Lot Like Baseball

Leveling up begins with doing the little stuff on a daily basis. Everyone is under the impression that big things happen when you set a high goal and hit a home run. But, you have to start by hitting a single. Granted, there's nothing exciting about just hitting a single—it doesn't get the same roar from the crowd that a home run does—but you'll win a lot more games and deals if you go for the single instead.

It's about strategy. Hitting a single puts everything in alignment. Start by setting up a deal you know you can do. For example, let's say your first deal is for $375,000. You get the clients set up for the deal by doing the preapproval for a buyer, or you get your seller set up for their listing. This puts the deal on the first base. Then, once things progress, the deal moves to second base.

With your first deal moving to second base, you set up your next single: a $275,000 deal. You get this transaction started, knowing that once the first deal moves to third base, you'll move this deal to second base. Second base in real estate means your buyer finds a house and puts down an offer or your seller has been given a serious offer to consider.

Now our first deal moves to third base: negotiations, funding, and the signing of contracts. Meanwhile, your second deal advances to second and your next deal ($350,000) moves to first base.

So the bases are loaded: $350,000 deal on first, $275,000 on second, and $375,000 on third. You have a total of $1 million in deals on the table. Now all you have to do is bring each transaction home and *keep* the bases loaded. You only have to advance one deal at a time instead of hitting home a huge deal at once.

Now, isn't that easier? Think about it: how much easier is it to get a deal for $250,000 or $300,000 than a deal for $1,000,000? All you have to do is work out the smaller deals and stack them up. Then, as each deal closes, you take home commissions more frequently, which creates a better quality of life for you.

Leveling Up Takes Teamwork

As you move from one step to the next in your deals, you'll need a team to help carry you home. This is where your trustworthy team members come in. These are your lenders, inspectors, appraisers, title companies, etc. As you move from base to base, they will be responsible for their end of the deal. And when you move from one step of the process to the next, you take these people with you. You'll always have deals for them. In return, they'll hit their own singles within your game (getting the inspection done, appraising the house, etc.) and bring your deals home more quickly.

If you follow this method, you'll never have empty bases. And you won't get sucked into trying to hit a big deal. You can make just as much money, if not more, by sticking to the singles. Remember, if you have multiple deals going, you'll never run out of business, and you'll survive.

Leveling Up Includes Daily Deposits

Leveling up isn't about going from 1 to 10. It's more like going from 1 to 1.1, then to 1.2, then to 1.3, and so on. Think Super Mario Brothers: there are eight worlds, and each world has four levels. You start at Level 1.1, and after you get to 1.4, you advance to Level 2.1, and so on. And if you try to skip levels, you won't get the points, the extra lives, or the coins needed to prepare you for Levels 8.1 through 8.4, the end of the game.

The same goes for life and your business. If you make getting to first base a priority, you'll get there. For me, getting to first base involves spending time with my family, working on my body, journaling, and working on my business. I do these things as deposits into my daily life, and they help me achieve my goals. I also understand that if I try to skip levels, I'll lose out on opportunities.

Each level is there to help you make it through and set you up for the next level. So if you do your daily deposits, you'll be ready for anything.

Everything Comes Full Circle When You Go Through Each Level

Every time you make it through a level, you literally level up. You go from just being an agent to being a better agent and eventually to being a leader. Leveling up also keeps your ego in check. You can't move from one challenge to the next if you have an ego problem. It's just not possible.

So now you know what to do. Stick to the singles. Don't go for the home run—you'll probably strike out. The goal in real estate isn't to hit the biggest deals all the time. Your goal is to stay in the game.

9

Don't Go Back to Being Normal

THE IMPORTANCE OF THE WORK we're doing here can't be overestimated. And I know it's a lot of work. Making a commitment to changing your life and growing is both exciting and extremely challenging. If you don't believe me, think about the last time you set a specific goal. A big one, one that was a high priority for you. When you set the goal, you made a commitment to it. You decided to put your time, money, and resources into it, and when things didn't quite work out, you had to summon extra energy so you could succeed. Or maybe you didn't finish it at all. Either way, the challenges persisted.

When this happens, don't turn back. Don't give in to the temptation of going back to normal. Even when things get really rough, don't go back.

The Realtor Code: Why Your Real Estate Career Is Slowly Dying And What You Can Do About It

There's a road map to keep you moving forward, and I've already given it to you. It's the daily deposits and the small stuff. These will keep you going in the right direction. But what happens when you get there? In our chapter about inner strength, we discussed having inner strength while on the path to creating the life and business you always wanted. But what happens when you reach your destination?

I've read tons of books on self-development. I've been to seminars and acted on the knowledge to get me to the Land of Riches. But no one really talks about the mountaintop. Reaching the ultimate goal. Cashing that commission check that makes a huge difference in your quality of life.

Your life will change, for sure, but how it changes is up to you.

The Rich Myth

I've been asked, "Mark, what are you going to do when you reach your multimillion-dollar goals?" I've never had that kind of money. I've done very well in real estate, but I've never had a super-big deal. It's not because I don't have what it takes to make that kind of deal happen. Over the years, my focus hasn't been on hitting a really high-commission goal (leveling up). I've put my efforts into setting up the right types of transactions that would continue to grow my business over the years. And it's worked.

But what if you really want to get into the multimillion-dollar deals? I have a theory: It doesn't matter if the transaction is for millions or just a couple of hundred thousand—the process is the same. If you don't want to backpedal, you have to invest in yourself.

Invest in Yourself: It's What Rich People Do

Many people think hitting it big in real estate will change their lives, but the only way to actually create the change is through investing. Right now, you're making an investment in yourself and your business by reading this book. And when you become successful, your investment will scale with the way your life changes. For example, let's say you want to start exercising. If you're poor, you start by doing push-ups, sit-ups, running, etc. You'd pick these exercises because they don't require purchasing expensive equipment or a gym membership. Then you make more money and you *can* join a gym. Eventually, you make enough money to hire a trainer, a nutritionist, and a few more people to help you get into shape.

People at their highest levels pay experts to help them succeed. They trust these people to manage their money, their business, and their time. They get advice from other successful people instead of their friends and family. And they don't throw all their money into external things.

Rich people understand that investing their money in the stock market, real estate, and other places takes away from investing in their own business endeavors. Yes, investing in those other areas will help them make more money, but they put themselves before anyone or anything else.

Sounds selfish, I know, but you can't help anyone else until you help yourself. You can't be an asset to other people until you have your own bearings.

Invest in Yourself and Become a Leader

I absolutely love LeBron James. Just like many other star athletes, LeBron had a certain amount of natural talent for basketball, but somewhere in his growing up, his mother encouraged his talents by allowing him to work closely with a local coach. This coach, among having other positive influences, helped LeBron become an all-star basketball player.

During his professional career, he eventually decided to leave his hometown team, the Cleveland Cavaliers, and the decision drew tons of scrutiny. Actually, to be frank, it pissed them off. They considered him a traitor.

While this was going on, LeBron was still working on his game. He was still getting his coaching and working on himself. And he kept winning. And winning. And winning. Most sports fans were shocked that he was able to do so well with all the adversity he was facing. But he did it. He continued to excel, rising above the negativity he was encountering. Then, in 2014, LeBron decided to go home to Cleveland, where he helped lead the Cavaliers to its first professional title in fifty-two years.

LeBron invested in himself, and it led him to a victory with his team. Even though he was considered a traitor, he was able to stay focused and succeed. In the end, his character, motivation, and willpower shone through. He never lost his focus on the game, and he brought back a win for his team.

You can be just like LeBron in your real estate game. Investing in yourself sets you up for becoming a leader in your life and the lives of others.

Investing in Yourself Makes You Dollars and Sense

I've spent *a lot* of money on coaching, but coaching has saved me so much money in the long run. When my life was falling apart—drinking all the time, ignoring my kids, on the verge of divorce, not taking responsibility for anything that happened to me—I was spending a ton of money. Wasting it. When I did the math, I realized that if I continued on that path, I'd spend tons more on therapy for myself and my family. And on medical bills due to my drinking. We're talking hundreds of thousands of dollars. But every dollar I've put into coaching has brought money back into my pocket. I'm thankful for that, because without the coaching, I wouldn't be here today.

Money can always be earned. If you need to pay for something, you'll find the money. But money doesn't change your mind-set. Investing in yourself changes your mind-set. If you don't change your mind-set, you won't make any other changes, and if you don't make those changes, who knows how much money you'll lose?

You Can Use Coaching to Invest in Literally Everything

When I take on a new challenge, I hire a coach. To write this book, I hired a coach. My coach is someone I've worked with on my content for a few years now. When we first sat down to write this book, I had a completely different direction in mind for it. My attitude and thoughts were very different then. My intentions were very different, too.

As I got further into my personal coaching, the book changed. Instead of being about me, this book became about you. My book coach helped me find the right words and stories to tell so that you could gain knowledge and learn how to create a better life. And in the end, by helping you, I'm helping myself. It's an investment in me that came full circle.

Rich People Invest So They Don't Become Top-Heavy

Before we close out this chapter, I want to touch on the small stuff again. Rich people make daily deposits into their lives (journaling, meditating, etc.). They do these things so that their foundation is strong, so that it's expanding and growing as their business and life expand. They do this because they get it.

When you make it to the top, you'll become top-heavy if you don't have a strong foundation. You'll fall because you don't have anything strong to stand on.

Make investing in yourself a priority. Put yourself first. You owe it to you.

10

A Scarcity Mind-set

ALL REAL ESTATE AGENTS ARE after one thing and one thing only: leads. Realtors want more leads because they lack the commitment to stay focused and do what they need to do. They'll ask for more and more leads, but they don't understand that they're not the only ones who need leads. If they work for a company or under a mortgage broker, that company needs leads as well. But that's not the issue. Realtors find themselves in these situations because they have a scarcity mind-set.

Where Does the Scarcity Mind-set Come From?

Realtors put themselves in scarcity mind-sets all the time. Let's say you have a buyer but they don't have a house they want to buy yet. The realtor will ask people for leads on houses and do everything they can to make it easier to get the leads. Suddenly, a deal comes through. Then the work stops. After the realtor gets paid, they become whimsical. If the leads come in, great. If they don't, there's nothing more he or she can do. They walk away with the belief that there's no work out there. And they develop a scarcity mind-set.

Your scarcity mind-set will cost you business. I've seen realtors put some effort into their business and wonder where they're falling short. They don't understand that they've fallen short from the beginning. They want listings, they expect listings, but they're in the business for the wrong reason. Yes, a listing means their name is out there for everyone to see, and it may bring in more business. But their head's not in the right place.

If you have ten listings for $100,000 each with a 3 percent commission, you might think you're walking away with $30,000, but that money doesn't exist until the sales go through. And if the deals fall through, you think you "lost" money. This also creates a scarcity mind-set. Any time you start depending on imaginary money, you'll constantly believe you never have enough money.

A Scarcity Mind-set Affects Your Entire Life

Some people use scarcity to overindulge, which affects multiple areas of their lives. Let's say you gave up drinking and you haven't had a drink in a while. Then, at a birthday party, you decide to have a drink. And since you haven't had a drink for some time, you end up getting a hangover. Having a hangover isn't fun, so you end up getting your favorite comfort food: a greasy, loaded cheeseburger. But guess what—it's gym day! And, of course, you don't have the energy or the willpower to get up and go.

A Scarcity Mind-set

So what did that drink cost you? Well, you had a hangover, you killed your diet, and you lost out on a chance to do something good for your body. You lost a lot.

When you overindulge, you do it because of scarcity. Since you haven't had a drink in a while, you get caught up in the celebration. If you don't drink often, you enjoy having something you don't have all the time. So be careful. Stay focused. Don't overindulge.

How Scarcity Leads to Greed

Most people don't see a connection between scarcity and greed, but the bond between them is tight. When I started organizing my coaching program, I thought about cost. How much should the program cost? What is its worth based on what the participants will receive? I could have charged $10,000 for my first large event. That would have been easy. But it didn't match up. Even though I was confident about the results, I knew I should be reasonable with the cost. When I say reasonable, I don't mean giving my services away for free or for a deep discount. I have something amazing to offer, something realtors could truly benefit from, and the price had to reflect that. So when I came up with a price, I felt good about it. I believed that both I and my realtors honored the price.

But let's say I didn't go that route. Let's say I decided to charge the $10,000 because I needed the money. But with my lack of experience, I failed to deliver at my very best because I was so focused on how much money I was making. But even with my inexperience, the event went okay. I got an excellent turnout,

The Realtor Code: Why Your Real Estate Career Is Slowly Dying And What You Can Do About It

and people spent more money on my coaching because they didn't quite get the breakthrough they were looking for without it. Everyone's pretty content except this one guy.

He felt taken advantage of because the information I shared didn't seem to be worth $10,000. So he sues me to get his money back. We get into a legal battle and it ends up costing me even more money than the $10,000.

Why did this happen? My scarcity mind-set had led to greed.

We see how scarcity and greed collide all the time. Look at lottery winners. Most people who win the lottery end up losing all their money within the first couple of years because they want everything they couldn't have before. The only people who seem to hold on to their money are the people who have to work for it. And as realtors, you have to work hard for your money.

When you build up your money over time, it changes you. You learn how to manage it better. Why? Because it forces you to move out of scarcity. As a good steward of your money, you won't have an urge to spend it.

The game is the same—we just play it differently. When you have only $10, you act like you have only $10. Everything is a struggle and costs too much. You become greedy with your $10 because it's all you have. But when you have a million dollars, you act like you have a million dollars. There's no reason to be greedy, because you can afford pretty much anything you want.

Now, I know there are people out there who think that a million dollars isn't enough. They would argue that someone with really high expenses wouldn't be able to manage on that little money. Or they might say that someone who makes a million dollars could decide to be greedy with their money because they want to. And that's true. But if you make a million dollars and you decide to be greedy, that's on you. It's not the money's fault—it's yours. And I bet that if you keep playing the money game like that, you won't have that money for long.

Beating Scarcity Comes Down to Doing the Work

I've said it over and over: you can't sweat the small stuff. And there's no way you can get around the small stuff, either. By doing the small stuff, you get prepped for the big stuff.

A realtor wants to sell million-dollar homes but hasn't sold one yet. He or she doesn't even live in a million-dollar home. You have to start by selling homes and living in homes within your budget. You have to become familiar with what that's like. You have to know how those buyers think. And as you move up, your clientele will move up, too.

You buy a half-million-dollar home and now you know what that process is like. You'll know what your buyers expect because you were one, too. People like to work with people who truly understand their needs. They buy from people who have the same level of certainty they do. It's not about the house they're buying—it's about how confident you are. And you can't have that confidence unless you've been there.

So Don't Try to Fake It Until You Make It. Actually Make It!

Don't let scarcity take you out. Don't let it keep you from having the things you want the way you want them. Have confidence in yourself. You're well on your way to becoming something amazing. Just do the work.

11

The Winning Play

IF YOU WANT TO BE successful, you start with your mind. You heal the way you think and start doing supporting acts to keep you moving forward. At this point, you should be in the right mind-set. The map to how your life works should be fairly clear. And if you've put the practices we've covered to good use, you should be seeing some good changes in your life.

But we can't stop there. I've taken you down the road to figuring out the small stuff, and now you should be working toward making your business profitable. In this chapter, I've outlined the five steps you need to take to create a profitable business and do the work that will bring in a fortune.

Step 1: Join a Successful Team

The turnover rate in real estate is high. Why is that? Realtors can be fake. They don't have true intentions. Most realtors are not in real estate for the right reasons. They want to make a ton of money instead of making sound, win-win deals.

Successful real estate teams are built by successful people. If you're working with a team, its members have probably been in the industry for a while. They understand how the small stuff works, and they know how to use it on a day-to-day basis. If you want to be good at your job, you have to work with the masters. If you try to do it all on your own, you'll fail.

The best leaders were the best followers—those who have taken what they learned to the next level. What exactly have they done?

Marketing: Every day when you post on Facebook, Twitter, Instagram, don't post about things that will make you feel significant. Instead, post about real estate. Be a person who shares valuable content that actually helps people. And when you're with other people, start a conversation. Ask them about their goals in real estate. Figure out what they want. And if they own a home, ask if they're ready to sell. You never know until you ask.

Open houses: Open houses may seem fruitless and boring, but do them anyway. You have to put out the signs, blow up the balloons, and sit there, waiting for someone to come. You have to do the work. That's how you get the 3 percent of prospects that other people won't. It's not easy, but it's worth it. You do the open houses and then, all of a sudden, here comes a $500,000 deal. Or maybe $1 million. You never know until you set up the balloons, take a seat, and wait to see who walks through that door.

A note about open houses: A successful team will give you tons of opportunities to do open houses. Take them. Continue to do them until you realize you don't have to do them anymore. If you pay close attention to the successful people on your team, you'll notice they don't have time to do the open houses.

If your pipeline is full, you probably won't need to do open houses for a long time. But don't fall into a scarcity mind-set. Keep your pipeline full, and if you have to jump back into doing open houses, build a plan before your pipeline dries out.

Stay mentally strong: Real estate isn't easy. People think it is, but it's not. It takes a lot of psychological preparation to stay on top of the game. You have buyers and their families telling you what to do, and you have sellers and their team telling you what they want you to do. Then there's the title company, inspection people and on and on.

It takes a village to close on a house. To endure having so many people tell you what to do and remain a sane person with your own thoughts is hard, but you can do it. The best people in real estate have strong minds. They work on themselves every day. All it takes is focus and being in the industry for the right reasons. All your hard work will pay off, guaranteed.

Step 2: Absorb Everything the Team Teaches You

What brought you into real estate? Were you running toward something or running away from it? If you need help answering this question, think about your job history. What were your other jobs like? Were you a top performer?

Getting into real estate for the wrong reasons is bad enough, but if you got into it because you struggled in all your other career fields, you're in for a rude awakening. If you have a horrible work ethic and horrible accountability, you'll suffer as a realtor. When it's completely on you to create a ton of work to be successful, you'll fail. The only way to get out of this is by making a decision today to shape up.

Start by working with your team and taking advantage of the things they do. The less sexy the task, the more profitable it will be. This includes open houses, daily social media posts, and creating a brand based on trust and integrity.

If the team uses a specific platform for prospecting, use it. If the team has dedicated call hours, call your prospects. Ask your team for tips on the best ways to communicate with your clients. Listen to them. Take the advice they give you on how you can do your job better. And stay accountable to your goals and your team's goals.

Step 3: Stay Away from Realtor-Inspired Happy Hours

This one is probably the most unpopular step of them all by far. As a new realtor, you'll be tempted to go to a happy hour put on by a mortgage or title company to meet other realtors. It can seem very inspiring. But it's a trap.

Happy hours are a waste of time, money, and energy. Successful agents don't go to these happy hours. They go to happy hours with other successful business owners. The realtors who go to realtor-focused happy hours tend to get caught up in the mob mentality. They trade war stories of being unproductive and unsuccessful. They get drunk and don't perform well in their businesses or their personal lives.

The only ones who benefit from these happy hours are the companies that put them on. The title or mortgage company hosting the happy hour is there to get new business from realtors. It's there to get new leads from realtors. The realtors don't get any leads from the hosting company. It's all a competition.

Think about it: do Walmart and Target get together for happy hour? Do they swap ideas on how they can help each other to get more business? No! If they do happy hours or company events, they do them internally. So if your team has a happy hour, go. But if you really want to jump into the realtor-inspired happy hours, go there with one intention only: to make an appearance. Attend these happy hours for a half an hour and then go to a different happy hour where you might be able to get more clients. Go to a doctor's happy hour and share your expertise on the real estate market, and then ask about their field. Don't dwell on trying to make a sale. Be knowledgeable and patient. The right moment will come.

Beware, new agents! Realtor-inspired happy hours are a big distraction. It's exciting to think you'll learn a thing of two from other realtors there, but trust me, you won't. In the end, you'll waste the little bit of money you have to show up and be demotivated.

When I was a new agent, I wasted hundreds of thousands of dollar (no joke) on these types of events. I'd go, drink, and pick up the tab for all the people left at the end. I'd spend tons of money "getting to know" these guys. And by drinking so much, I gained weight, which led me to hire a trainer, and so forth. Plus, I was so hung over all the time that I lost out on deals.

Don't do it. Don't go to the happy hours. Put your money and time into something that will invest back in you.

Step 4: Working the Phone

When you're in the office, answer the phone. Most real estate offices have a generic number on the sign. Agents will get an opportunity to sit by the phone for a block of time and wait for potential clients to call in. Get with a successful team that offers floor time on the phones. Take as much as possible. If you answer the phone, you'll get the lead.

It's really that simple. Sit by the phone and pick it up when someone calls. You'd be surprised by how many agents don't take advantage of the available phone time. Don't be like them — be willing to sit there for your allotted time and wait. Patiently. Trust me, you'll be glad you did.

So, what do you say when someone calls in? Ask for a script. Many of the bigger teams offer phone training and scripts you can use. Don't miss out on these opportunities just because you feel unprepared.

Step 5: Learn the Mortgage Side

Real estate deals live and die in the mortgage process. The only way you'll make money in this business is by getting your buyers and sellers through the deal. The alternative is kind of like buying a car without putting gas in it. Without gas, the car is just metal on rubber. It just sits there. So does a house that doesn't have a mortgage attached to it.

Most realtors don't have a say in where the house goes under contract. That's the client's decision. But the client does need the realtor to open the doors to the home so they can see it (open houses, showings, etc.). This is your golden opportunity to teach your prospects about the mortgage side. And you can also see if they're truly ready to make the purchase or sale.

I know a realtor who was working with a couple to get them preapproved for a mortgage, but they didn't get approved because the husband had no credit. The realtor didn't quite understand the mortgage side, so she focused on showing the family houses instead of fixing the situation.

In this example, the realtor could have directed the client to add her husband onto one of her credit cards for a year, which would have built up his credit score. And in the meantime, she could have worked on all the other areas of the mortgage process the client would need to know before buying the house. She wasted valuable time showing houses when she could have focused on learning the mortgage side and sharing it with her clients.

Knowledge is power and money in this industry. You can never have too much.

Your Final Step: Just Do the Work

Your job as a realtor is to show houses and make good deals for your clients. You have to do the work. If you follow the five steps above, you'll be well on your way to surviving and thriving in this business. You'll become a leader, full of knowledge and in possession of a strong work ethic. You'll be an example for everyone on your team. And most important, you'll get paid!

12

What the Future Holds for You

THE BEAUTY OF DOING REAL estate isn't giving service. It's not about driving around and helping indecisive people figure out what they want. And it's not about working long hours, communicating with tons of business partners, and fighting hard for commissions. The beauty of it is the ability to use real estate in your future. You can learn how to flip houses, buy commercial properties, and use real estate as a passive income. Then, once you're ready to retire, you can sell your properties for a nice chunk of change.

I don't know if you've realized this already, but the end game for realtors should be to use the industry to make as much money as they can. It's kind of like working out. Some people work out to get six-pack abs, while others work out because they want a particular lifestyle. Those who make it a lifestyle are looking for many ways to stay healthy and strong. In return, their bodies become better, and they eventually get to the point where they can eat whatever they want and it barely affects them.

As a realtor, you can get in your best shape if you use all your training and knowledge on yourself. You're the first to know what's going on in the market. And you know how it will affect not only your business but also your personal real estate goals. You can use this information to advance your goals and the goals of your clients, but you have to be in the right mind-set.

There are two types of realtors: service realtors and investment realtors. Let's talk about what makes them different and how you can shift your thinking from that of a service agent to that of an investment agent.

Service Realtors

Most people start out as service realtors simply because they don't know any better. If you join a team, its members will push you to learn the ropes and how to give the best service. Your main focus will be getting the training down and learning how you can apply it to get some houses sold.

Being a service realtor is hard because you have to deal with people and their emotions. When someone picks a house, they aren't thinking about the structure. They aren't romanced by the amount of money they can save in taxes every year by being a homeowner. None of that is really important. Your clients fall in love with what the house represents. And just like anyone else looking for love, they'll ride a roller coaster of emotions until they find the house that's everything they hoped for. And you, the realtor, ride this roller coaster with them. It's your job to keep them motivated and sane as they zap all the energy out of you.

This probably isn't the life you want. You didn't get into real estate to devote the best years of your life to being an emotional counselor with potential homeowners. You want money. You want freedom. And for that, you have to become an investment realtor.

Investment Realtors

You don't have to start out as a service realtor. You can become an investment realtor right out the gate. Your first task is to get very clear on what your goals in real estate are. How much money do you want to retire with? How long do you want to work? These are a couple of things to consider. Then, once you get clear on your goals, find the best team. Absorb everything the members teach you. Get busy doing the work and putting everything you learn into practice.

During your learning, you'll notice that the most successful people in real estate are constantly looking for investment properties. They have an "in" to the luxury lifestyle, and they know how to make more money. They have conviction about what they want, and you should, too. The most lucrative route in real estate is to become an investment realtor.

The Biggest Reward for Investment Realtors

Investment realtors don't chase money. They don't set goals around getting a certain number of deals so they can roll in the big leads. They have one thing on their minds: self-sustainability. When you're able to sustain on your own, you have true freedom. You have the ability to design your business in any way you want. And as you grow your business, it will start to do the work for you. That's how the big players do it.

As an investment realtor, you'll land bigger deals. You may start by buying a property or two, and as you get more money, you'll move on to more properties and maybe even an apartment complex. Either way, your growing knowledge of the business will give you opportunities to make bigger deals happen.

Commercial Real Estate

There's one last area of real estate I need to touch on: commercial real estate. Playing in the commercial space is unique. Everything is done based on business, not emotions. And the payouts are a lot higher. A "broke" commercial agent is pulling in about $500,000 a year. It's by far the highest-paid job in our industry, and it comes with its own set of rules.

Doing commercial real estate requires great patience. Most agents do a ton of work to land only about two deals a year. So if you want to step into this park, you need to have plenty of money on hand or another income stream to tide you over.

Most agents who get into commercial real estate developed a strong service base and then moved into the investment arena.

After they've mastered that, they go into commercial real estate. It's about building a strong, balanced portfolio.

Building Your Own Team

Don't get caught up in mastering just service real estate. Don't focus so heavily on the end game. These things won't give you more time and freedom in your business. The final step to becoming a true investment realtor is creating your own team.

You have to build your own team so you don't have to do so much work. This will allow you to delegate and free up more of your time. But as you build your team, don't try to rush into the next thing. There is no end. There is no finish line. You have to continuously evolve and let your team evolve with you. Enjoy the time you have with them and the sense of accomplishment. After all, you were able to elevate the lives of those around you!

Staying In the Moment

It takes most realtors about two years to see any type of success, but if you work with a strong team, you may be able to shrink this time frame. You may spend the first five years of your career as a service agent, though.

Don't freak out—there's no set amount of time for you to stay in any particular role. Everything depends on you and how hard you're willing to work. The more you apply the lessons in this book, the faster you'll move forward. You'll have more opportunities to make more money. The leads will come in much faster. And you'll build up your pipeline faster, close more deals, and get better leads.

But this book doesn't just apply to your work life. You can use these principles in your day-to-day life, too. And since real estate is so hard, if you can succeed here, you can succeed in anything. Remember, real estate is the biggest lie—people think it's easy. The truth is, the fact that you're still in it should be recognized and honored.

If you've made it through this book, you're already proving you can do hard things and win. I'm honored that you're here, and you should be, too. You've shown you can do this, and you should be rewarded for all your hard work.

Real estate is hard, and you just conquered it! Well-done!

Conclusion: We Got This!

SO, HERE WE ARE, AT the end of this part of our journey together. We've covered a lot in this book, but the story doesn't end here. This book is meant to serve as the first step to making a major change in your life. A way for you to get back to basics and begin again.

At the end of the day, real estate is a people game. Buying a home is one of the most understated commodities a person can own. And even though technology makes it easy for buyers and sellers to enter the marketplace, your clients don't want to go through the process alone. They need you—the best version of who you are today and who you'll be tomorrow. But you can't do it by yourself.

It's impossible to master the game of real estate on your own. It's not because you're not strong, nor is it tied to your ability to work hard. The fact is, you need a guide, someone to give you courage as you learn and master this craft.

Navigating through Challenges

We all have challenges, no matter how well we're doing in life, but there's nothing worse than going through your experiences alone. Now, I know what you're thinking: *I have family and friends to help me when I'm feeling down.* That's probably true, but being a realtor causes your problems to shift. Now instead of just managing your life issues, you have business issues that can be hard to navigate, too. This can be overwhelming.

I'm sure you've had days when you thought about giving up. When you thought about all your talents and abilities and all the other things you could be doing instead of real estate. It's for those days you need guidance. You need a person to champion you until you achieve whatever you think is impossible. That's where coaching comes in.

Coaching Gives You the Advantage

If you peel back the layers of what realtors do, you'll soon realize that all realtors do the same thing: buy and sell houses. They market the same and target the same types of clients. Some are better than others, but in the end, what you do is no different from what your competition does. So, to get the advantage, you need coaching.

Coaching gets you to the end of the game. It cultivates your inner strength and boosts your endurance. It frees you from the constant procrastination and low-productivity cycles other realtors are caught in every day. Coaching gives you freedom. It allows you to be different.

Being Different

The work I do with realtors isn't about what they should do but rather who they should be. Your clients want to connect with someone who's different from everyone else. They want to be kindred to someone who knows who they are and what they want. By working with me, I can make you that difference they're looking for.

When we work together, it's not about teaching you how to fake it before you make it. It's not a plea to get you to see something in me that will persuade you to give me your money. The work we have to do together is so much more important than that. It's about the sweet victory of greatness!

At this point, you've done enough to keep you in the game, but now it's time for you to see what it's like to be great.

The Great Realtor Life

Some realtors think you have to have million-dollar listings to have a great life as a realtor. Would you believe me if I told you that you could be great today no matter where you are in your career?

Successful realtors lead every aspect of their lives. They begin today because they know tomorrow holds nothing but great things for them. They worked with their coach to carve out their exact intention in life, the impression they will make on other people. They chose one day to make that day different, and then everything changed.

Make Today Different

In the next twenty-four hours, I invite you to give coaching with me a try. Stand in your power, declare that today will be different, and commit to the better version of yourself.

I believe you can do it. I believe you have a real chance at a great life. And if you believe that, too, let's do this. You have twenty-four hours to make the call. And the clock starts now!

Quick Reference Guide

This quick reference guide will help you on a day-to-day basis. I recommend referring to it every day for the next year to check on the progress you've made. Use it when you feel like you're losing your way. If that's not enough, go back and read more on the topic.

Loyalty and Trust...Making Yourself Good for Business

The obstacle most realtors face is lack of integrity in the industry. To combat this, you have to take an honest inventory of your life and ask, "Am I loyal and trustworthy?"

Becoming Loyal and Trustworthy

- **Focus on authenticity.** Be conscious of who you are and what you stand for, and work only with people in the industry who share your values.
- **When you make a mistake, claim it and move on.** If you make a mistake, don't try to cover it up or lie about it. Claim it, fix it, and move on.

- **Don't miss the details.** Don't rush through the process to make money. Pay close attention to the details, and double-check your work.
- **Promote win-win situations.** Your intentions should promote relationships where you and your partners support one another.
- **Don't break promises, not even to yourself.** If you say you're going to do something, do it. And if you can't, be truthful about it.
- **Examine your goals.** Do your goals support loyalty and trustworthiness? If not, adjust them until they do.

Breaking the Procrastination Cycle

The real estate world breeds procrastination because agents think getting a bigger listing will bring them better chances of making money. You can break this cycle by doing the following:

- **Do the small stuff.** Get up early, eat consistently and well, avoid excessive drinking, and get to bed early. These small, simple lifestyle tweaks will help you stay in the game long enough to make serious money.
- **Stay motivated.** Motivation builds up when you can first handle having a day-to-day routine you've mastered. Then, when you move up to the bigger stuff, you'll have the motivation to take it on.
- **Focus on self-discipline and gratitude.** Self-discipline brings you the right energy to create gratitude.
- **Don't feel entitled.** Never have a sense that someone owes you anything in this business.

Quick Reference Guide

Building Endurance

Real estate is one of the most lucrative industries, but it can be hard to make it a long-lasting career. You can build up your endurance through dedication and a strong work ethic.

Here are a few things you can do to demonstrate your work ethic:

- **Prospect.** Consistently prospect.
- **Follow up.** Follow up on every lead and in a timely manner.
- **Follow through.** When you make a commitment, follow through.
- **Be accountable.** Stay accountable to your goals and make progress!

Making Sound Business Decisions

Sound business decisions keep your business alive and give it the endurance to withstand any market. Right now, I want you to take the steps on the following list:

- **Look at your schedule.** How much of your day is spent doing what?
- **Check on your goals.** What goals have you set for the year? When will you achieve them?
- **Track your expenses.** Are you spending too much money on this and not enough money on that?
- **Plan your next move.** What's the next move in your business? Why did you choose this action, and how will it benefit you?

Creating Your Vision

Create a vision for each area of your life—body, mind, purpose and business—and break each vision into ninety-day challenges.

- **Body Vision:** Set up a ninety-day challenge to increase your daily activities and implement a healthy eating plan.
- **Mind Vision:** Set up a ninety-day challenge to focus on building up your mental toughness around prospecting and learning more about both our industry and money management.
- **Purpose Vision:** Set up a ninety-day challenge to live each day with purpose and intention.
- **Business Vision:** Within the next ninety days, set up a strong vision for your business by taking the following steps:

    o **Step 1: Add Value by Staying Connected**
    How will you remain relevant and add value to your business and those around you?

    o **Step 2: Get Clear on What You Want**
    Don't focus on the money. Instead, find out what else propels you in your career.

    o **Step 3: Practice Gratitude**
    List ways you can be grateful and continue to be grateful in your business.

    o **Step 4: Say No**
    If something doesn't fit into your vision, don't include it.

o **Step 5: Add Coaching**
Your vision cannot be completely executed unless you have someone to hold you accountable.

Cultivating Inner Strength

We need inner strength to give us that extra push to go from good to great. Realtors lose inner strength, so you must cultivate it every day. Here's how to cultivate it:

- **Start with confidence.** The more confidence you have, the easier it will be to start building your inner strength.
- **Don't give in to arrogance.** When you start working on your confidence, don't let your arrogance steal your humility.
- **Use a twelve-month journal to track your progress.** Capture all the things that happen in your business. After a while, you'll realize you're stronger than you thought.
- **Focus on longevity.** Use your longevity to consistently grow each year.

Evolution and Framework

When things aren't working out, you have to evolve and create a new framework. Here's the best way to create the perfect framework in your business:

- **Set a frame.** People operate well in this environment because it sets boundaries; your job is to keep these boundaries and enforce them.

- **Enforce boundaries.** Set these boundaries with your clients:
    - **Preapprovals.** Your buyers must get preapproval before you go out to look at houses.
    - **Proper Documentation.** Make sure your clients give you the right paperwork early on in the process.
    - **Expectations.** By setting a boundary around your client's expectations, you'll cut down on all the guesswork.
- **Get proper guidance.** Hire a coach to help with your evolution as a realtor.

Leveling Up Beats Scarcity

Leveling up is about strategy. Put one deal on the plate and then move on to the next. Use teamwork (lenders, agents, inspectors, appraisers, etc.) to bring your deals home. Be sure to make daily deposits into your business so you can continue playing the game without falling into a scarcity mind-set.

Practice Investing

Invest in yourself and your business. The best way to invest in yourself is to hire a coach. Many of the greatest athletes and successful people have coaches who hold them accountable to their goals and dreams. Investing in yourself gives you the ability to invest in your business and your entire team.

Quick Reference Guide

The Winning Play

Building a successful career as a realtor comes down to doing the work and doing it to the absolute best of your ability. Here's how to do that:

- **Step 1: Join a Successful Team.** Successful real estate teams are built by successful people. Absorb everything they have to teach you.
- **Step 2: Market.** Be a person who shares valuable content that actually helps people.
- **Step 3: Hold Open Houses.** You have to put out the signs, blow up the balloons, and sit there so you can get the 3 percent of prospects that other people won't.
- **Step 4: Stay Mentally Strong.** The best people in real estate have strong minds. They work on themselves every day.
- **Step 5: Stay Away from Realtor-Inspired Happy Hours.** The only people who benefit from these happy hours are the companies that put them on.
- **Step 6: Work the Phone.** Get with a successful team that offers floor time on the phones. Take as much as possible.
- **Step 5: Learn the Mortgage Side.** Real estate deals live and die in the mortgage process. The only way you'll make money in this business is by getting your buyers and sellers through the deal.

What the Future Holds for You

There are two different types of realtors: service realtors and investment realtors. If you want to make a long, lucrative career in real estate, move from being just a service realtor and set your sights higher.

- **Become an investment realtor.** Investment realtors don't chase money. They have one thing on their minds: self-sustainability. When you're an investment realtor, your deals are bigger.
- **Consider commercial real estate.** All deals done in commercial real estate come down to business, not emotions. And the payouts are a lot higher. A "broke" commercial agent is pulling in about $500,000 a year. But beware: doing commercial real estate requires a lot of patience.
- **Build your own team.** True investment realtors creating their own teams. This allows you to delegate and free up more of your time.

www.ingramcontent.com/pod-product-compliance
Lightning Source LLC
LaVergne TN
LVHW011427080426
835512LV00005B/304